BRAVE THE BIOME
OCEAN
[SURVIVAL GUIDE]

[CYNTHIA O'BRIEN]

CRABTREE
PUBLISHING COMPANY
WWW.CRABTREEBOOKS.COM

BRAVE THE BIOME

Author: Cynthia O'Brien

Editors: Sarah Eason, Jennifer Sanderson, and Ellen Rodger

Proofreader and indexer: Tracey Kelly

Proofreader: Petrice Custance

Editorial director: Kathy Middleton

Design: Jessica Moon

Cover design: Tammy McGarr

Photo research: Rachel Blount

Production coordinator and Prepress technician: Tammy McGarr

Print coordinator: Katherine Berti

Consultant: David Hawksett

Produced for Crabtree Publishing by Calcium

Photo Credits:
t=Top, c=Center, b=Bottom, l= Left, r=Right

Inside: Jessica Moon: p. 13b; Shutterstock: Aaronejbull87: pp. 12–13; Brett Allen: p. 32; ArtMari: p. 7t; Cameris: p. 6t; Rich Carey: pp. 18–19; Evgo1977: p. 25; FtLaud: pp. 20–21; Lyu Hu: p. 17t; Ihor Hvozdetskyi: p. 19t; Liya Blumesser: pp. 30–31; Marcutti: pp. 22–23; Motortion Films: pp. 16–17, 29b; Murattellioglu: p. 5t; N.K. Photography: p. 14b; Nejron Photo: pp. 14–15; Tyler Olson: p. 10b; Andrey Polivanov: pp. 4–5; RavenEyePhoto: p. 4b; Viktorija Reuta: p. 11t; Sue Robinson: pp. 28–29; Jean-Edouard Rozey: p. 13t; Sata Production: p. 9b; Skynavin: p. 7b; Okawa Somchai: pp. 6–7; Steve Photography: pp. 26–27; Stockphoto-graf: p. 28t; TheBlackRhino: p. 23b; Bodor Tivadar: pp. 17b, 19b; Sergey Uryadnikov: pp. 24–25; Paul Vasarhelyi: pp. 10–11; Richard Whitcombe: p. 24; David Wingate: p. 23t; Andrey Yurlov: pp. 8–9.

Cover: All images from Shutterstock

Library and Archives Canada Cataloguing in Publication

Title: Ocean survival guide / Cynthia O'Brien.
Names: O'Brien, Cynthia (Cynthia J.), author.
Description: Series statement: Brave the biome | Includes index.
Identifiers: Canadiana (print) 20200286293 |
  Canadiana (ebook) 20200286331 |
  ISBN 9780778781356 (softcover) |
  ISBN 9780778781295 (hardcover) |
  ISBN 9781427125750 (HTML)
Subjects: LCSH: Survival at sea—Juvenile literature. |
  LCSH: Survival—Juvenile literature. |
  LCSH: Ocean—Juvenile literature.
Classification: LCC GF86 .O27 2021 | DDC j613.6/909162—dc23

Library of Congress Cataloging-in-Publication Data

Names: O'Brien, Cynthia (Cynthia J.), author.
Title: Ocean survival guide / Cynthia O'Brien.
Description: New York : Crabtree Publishing Company, [2021] |
  Series: Brave the biome | Includes index.
Identifiers: LCCN 2020029915 (print) | LCCN 2020029916 (ebook) |
  ISBN 9780778781295 (hardcover) |
  ISBN 9780778781356 (paperback) |
  ISBN 9781427125750 (ebook)
Subjects: LCSH: Survival at sea--Juvenile literature. |
  Shipwreck survival--Juvenile literature.
Classification: LCC G525 .O27 2021 (print) | LCC G525 (ebook) |
  DDC 613.6/909162--dc23
LC record available at https://lccn.loc.gov/2020029915
LC ebook record available at https://lccn.loc.gov/2020029916

Crabtree Publishing Company

www.crabtreebooks.com   1-800-387-7650

Printed in the U.S.A./092020/CG20200810

Published in Canada
Crabtree Publishing
616 Welland Ave.
St. Catharines, Ontario
L2M 5V6

Published in the United States
Crabtree Publishing
347 Fifth Ave.
Suite 1402-145
New York, NY 10016

Published in the United Kingdom
Crabtree Publishing
Maritime House
Basin Road North, Hove
BN41 1WR

Published in Australia
Crabtree Publishing
3 Charles Street
Coburg North
VIC, 3058

CONTENTS

The world's oceans and seas cover about 70 percent of Earth's surface. They range from the icy waters of the polar regions to warm, tropical seas. Underneath the surface, the ocean is buzzing with life. Whales, fish, coral, and many more living things make their homes in this salty **biome**. Exploring the oceans is thrilling, but it can also be tough. Powerful **currents**, icebergs, and storms can challenge even experienced sailors.

WIDE-OPEN WATERS

The Pacific is the largest of Earth's five oceans. It stretches from the Arctic Ocean in the north to the Southern Ocean around Antarctica. The western Pacific Ocean has the most **typhoon** activity. This is because its waters are warm. The Indian Ocean is also warm. It experiences **monsoons**. Doing some research about the oceans—including finding out when storms might be likely—is vital before undertaking any trip on ocean waters.

Navigation, or finding one's way, is a key survival skill on the open sea. Sailors must be able to navigate in even the wildest weather.

SURVIVING POLAR OCEANS

Earth's coldest places lie in the Arctic and Southern Oceans. There, sheets of thick ice cover much of the ocean surface. Icebergs can hold hidden dangers because much of their ice lies below the water's surface, making it dangerous for boats that travel in polar oceans. In both oceans, ice caps are now melting and breaking due to climate change. Climate change is the gradual change in Earth's climate.

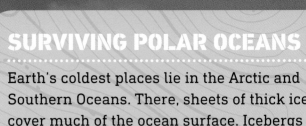

Arctic Ocean iceberg

LOOK OUT!

Look for the "How to Survive" and "Be Prepared" features in this book. These list many of the techniques that people have used to survive on oceans.

5

There are many things to think about before taking a boat out on the ocean. Taking a course in ocean survival skills is crucial. Understanding how to use the radio if someone needs to call for help is also important, and so is looking at maps and checking the weather before setting out. Sailors need to think about what to pack for all situations. Accidents at sea can lead to injuries to people and damage to boats. It is necessary to have equipment on board to deal with these emergencies if they happen.

MAKE A PLAN

A float plan is a plan put in writing before sailors embark on their trip. It has a list with details of everyone on board a boat and emergency contact numbers. It also contains information about the boat, the sailors' intended route, and details about the boat's signal and communication devices, such as radios. Leaving the float plan with someone on land can help in locating the boat in case of an emergency.

A float plan has the marked route that a sailor or sailing group will take.

SAFETY AT SEA

Taking enough drinking water on board a boat can make the difference between life and death. A good rule is to bring about 1 gallon (3.8 liters) per person per day. Sailors need to dress for the weather. The Sun can be strong when out on open water, so during the day, it is better to wear long-sleeved T-shirts and hats to avoid sunburn. Good sunglasses keep harmful sun rays from damaging the eyes. Often, it will be cold at night, so blankets must be kept on board. Extra clothes in case others get wet is also useful.

BE PREPARED

It is important to make a checklist of things to pack. These are essential items:

- cell phone
- first aid kit
- compass
- maps
- watch
- tool kit
- duct tape
- two buckets, one smaller than the other
- plastic sheeting
- mirror
- knife
- flashlight
- batteries

compass ·····

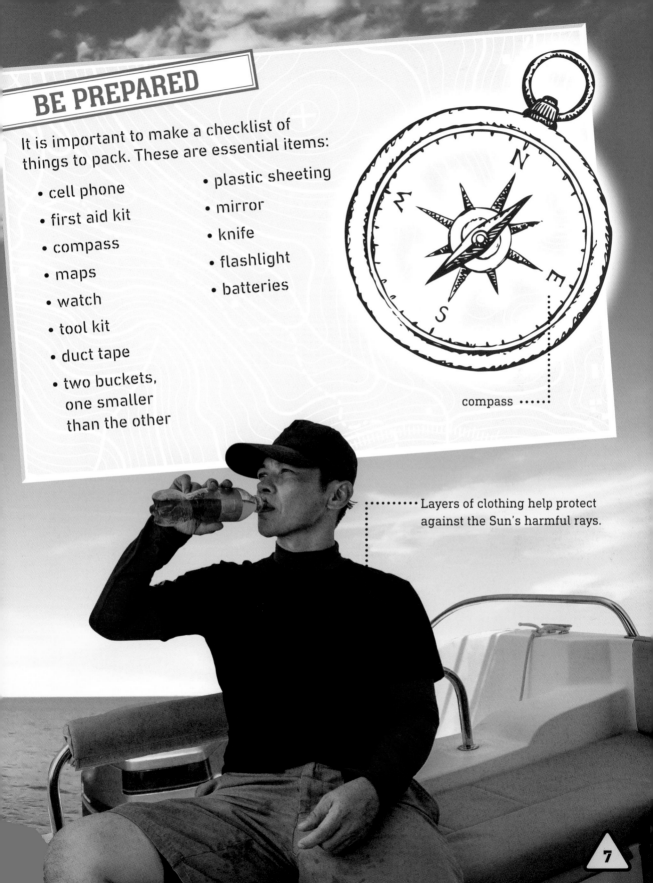

········ Layers of clothing help protect against the Sun's harmful rays.

SMASHED BY A HURRICANE:
TAMI ASHCRAFT

In 1983, Tami Oldham Ashcraft and her fiancé Richard Sharp were sailing from Tahiti to San Diego, California, to deliver a yacht named the *Hazana* to its owner. Two weeks into the trip, they heard over the radio that a storm had started near Panama. Tami and Richard tried to steer north, but Hurricane Raymond swallowed them up. The huge 50-foot (15 m) waves and violent winds tossed the *Hazana* up and over.

ALONE AT SEA

Tami opened her eyes about 27 hours later. She was in the yacht's cabin, surrounded by water. The force of the hurricane had knocked her unconscious, badly injuring her head. Dazed, Tami made her way to the deck, but Richard was gone. The waves had swept him overboard. Tami was alone on the wrecked yacht in the middle of the Pacific Ocean.

MAYDAY!

Tami sent out Maydays, which are distress signals, but no one heard her. She realized that she would have to try and navigate the yacht to the closest shore. This was 1,500 miles (2,414 km) away in Hilo, Hawaii. The storm had damaged all the yacht's equipment, so Tami had just a **sextant** and her watch to guide her. Tami was determined to survive. She pumped out the water and tried to get the yacht's engine going, but nothing worked.

Tami had to rely on the wind and ocean currents to move the *Hazana* forward. She rigged up the small storm sail and used the sail and a broken pole to steer the yacht north. Using her watch and sextant, Tami found the strong North **Equatorial** Current, hoping this would carry the boat to Hilo. She knew this was her only chance to get to safety.

LAND AHEAD

As she drifted along on her own, Tami searched the skies and water for help. She sent up **flares** when she caught sight of two ships in the distance, but no one saw them. A military plane also flew over, but the pilot did not spot the yacht. After more than a month, and with hardly any food and water left, Tami was close to giving up hope.

After 41 days, Tami saw the lights of Hilo Harbor in the early morning. She waited until it was light so that she could move forward safely. On the way into the harbor, Tami sent up flares. This time, the people on a ship saw the flares. The ship slowed down and moved toward the *Hazana*. Its crew called the Coast Guard to tow the *Hazana* into the harbor. Tami was saved at last and had survived her ordeal at sea.

It is important for all sailors to understand ocean currents. If a boat's sails fail, sailors must rely on the movements of currents to carry them forward. Tami's knowledge of the seas helped her travel to safety.

Shipwrecks, capsized boats, and falling overboard are all **hazards** of ocean exploration. If people are stranded in the water, this can cause panic, and they will not be able to think clearly or breathe properly. In these emergency situations, it is very important to stay calm. It is also important to keep the body moving and afloat until help comes.

HOLD ON

All boats must have life jackets or personal flotation devices (PFDs) on board for every person. If the seas become stormy and there is any chance of the boat capsizing, or turning over, everyone must put on a life jacket. If someone falls into the water, they must look for a **dinghy**, raft, swim ring, or anything that floats, and swim toward it. A pair of pants can also be turned into a float: a knot is tied in each pant leg, then air is blown into the legs to make a flotation device.

Panicking in the water is one of the most dangerous things a person can do. It is very important to always remain calm.

swim ring

HOW TO HANDLE COLD WATER

Hypothermia is a condition where the body loses heat faster than it can produce it. This can happen quickly if a person is stranded in the water, because the body loses heat faster in the water than it does in the air. A life jacket or even some clothes will help to **preserve** heat. They will also help the body stay warmer by keeping more of it afloat and out of the water.

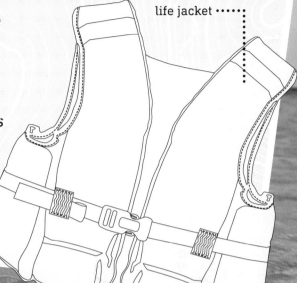

life jacket

THE RIGHT MOVES

People who have to stay for a long time in the water need to move their bodies to suit the water temperature and speed. For example, in calm water, floating on their backs and breathing slowly is best because it saves energy. In rough seas, using the breaststroke and treading water helps keep the body afloat without using too much energy.

Swimming is tiring. When a rest is needed, the easiest position is for a person to stretch out their arms, hold their breath, and let their head fall back and under the water. The rest of the body will float upward. To come up for air, the person moves their legs and arms a little, raises their head, breathes in and out, then goes back to the resting position.

Out on the ocean, the Sun can feel very hot. To help it keep cool, the body loses water through sweating. However, sweating **dehydrates** the body, making people feel thirsty. Dehydration is dangerous because water is more important than food for the body to work properly. Without water, no one can survive for a long period of time.

HOLD THE SALT

It may be tempting to drink ocean water, but this is a very dangerous thing to do. Seawater contains a lot of salt. If drunk, the water's salt dehydrates the body quickly and also makes people feel very thirsty. They are then likely to drink even more salt water to deal with the thirst. The kidneys, which are the organs that handle salt, cannot process the extra salt and can fail.

Turtles can provide water and food, but many types of sea turtles are **endangered**, so they should be hunted only in an emergency.

FINDING WATER

Rainwater is the best source of drinking water when at sea, and it is safe to drink. To collect it, watch the clouds, and always be ready to collect rain when it falls, even at night. Fish eyes contain water, as do the blood and meat of turtles and birds. Eating these will help the body keep hydrated.

HOW DO FISH DO IT?

Fish and sea birds survive in salt water because their bodies are specially **adapted**. Fish take in water through their skin and **gills**, then their kidneys and gills get rid of it. Sea birds, such as penguins and seagulls, drink salt water. A gland at the top of the beak, behind the eye, then pumps the salt from the water out through the nostrils.

gills

HOW TO MAKE FRESH WATER

It is possible to make fresh water from salt water. This process is called desalination. To do this, place some salt water in a bucket or large bowl. Then, a second, smaller container into the larger one. The smaller container must be weighed down. Everything should be covered with some plastic or other waterproof material, securing it with string. Another weight should be added in the middle of the plastic, over the smaller container. When in the Sun, the salt water will **evaporate**. Then, it will **condense** on the plastic covering. This fresh water will drip into the smaller container.

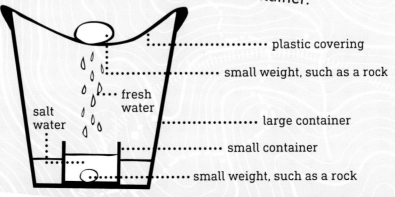

plastic covering

small weight, such as a rock

fresh water

salt water

large container

small container

small weight, such as a rock

LONE SURVIVOR:
JOSÉ SALVADOR ALVARENGA

José Salvador Alvarenga and Ezequiel Córdoba fished for a living. They set out from the coast of Mexico in mid-November, 2012. In a short time, the two caught enough fish to fill a large crate. Then a storm hit. José tried to steer the boat back to shore, but waves lashed at the low-lying boat, filling it with water. Ezequiel bailed, or scooped out, the water as fast as he could, but soon the boat's motor sputtered to a stop.

LOSING CONTACT

As the storm raged around them, José had to make some quick decisions. The water had ruined the **GPS** tracker, but the radio was still working, so José called for help. They had no anchor, so the men tied **buoys** to the sides. Still, the waves continued to turn, lift, and drop the boat. Then, the radio went silent. José did not have a backup battery, so he had no way of contacting anyone.

Filling an empty plastic bottle with rainwater can provide a vital source of water in an emergency situation.

ADRIFT AT SEA

Before their trip, José had loaded the boat with supplies, including ice and gallons of gas. These and the catch of fish made the boat heavy and unstable. The men decided to toss all of this overboard. They also threw the radio, engine, and GPS into the ocean. Then, they huddled together in the empty shell of the boat to keep warm. With no engine or sails, the boat drifted with the current. The men had no control over where it was going, and they had no idea where they were.

To survive, José caught fish with his hands. The men ate the fish raw or dried it in the Sun. They used anything they could find to catch rainwater, even plastic bottles they found in the sea. After about two months, Ezequiel became very weak. José had no way to save him, and Ezequiel died.

WASHED ASHORE

As the months went by, José kept alive by drinking rainwater and eating whatever fish he could catch. The longer José drifted, the more hopeless he felt. José could not believe his eyes when, one day, he spotted land. In one last desperate move, José cut away the buoys, so that the current could carry the boat closer to shore. When the shore was close enough to reach by swimming, José jumped into a wave and let it wash him onto the beach. José had reached one of the tiny Marshall Islands, far southwest of Hawaii. Only two people live on the island. They fed José and called for help to get him off the island. Altogether, José had spent 438 days drifting at sea—but he survived to tell his story.

If a boat sinks or capsizes, it is always safer to stay near the capsized or sunken boat. Rowing away in a dinghy can be dangerous unless people know exactly where they are going. If there is another ship or boat nearby, it is best not to try and swim or row toward it. Instead, a Visual Distress Signal (VDS) device must be used. These devices will alert the crew of the ship to the problem. VDS devices can also show the location of a boat lost at sea.

VISUAL SIGNALS

VDS devices can be **pyrotechnic**, such as flares, or nonpyrotechnic, such as lights and flags. By law, there must be six pyrotechnic devices on board or two nonpyrotechnic devices. The right signal must be used at the right time. For example, smoke flares, are used during the day. These flares are handheld or float on the water and release orange smoke for a few minutes. Waving an orange flag is also an effective daytime signal. Red flares work as signals during the day or night. Flares must never be fired into the wind. A distress signal, or **SOS**, can also be used to attract attention. These are three quick flashes of light or blasts of a horn, followed by three longer flashes or blasts, and three quick flashes or blasts.

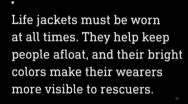

Life jackets must be worn at all times. They help keep people afloat, and their bright colors make their wearers more visible to rescuers.

FISH LIGHTS

Deep under the ocean's surface, it is very dark. At least 1,500 types of fish use bioluminescence to communicate, find **prey**, or for defense against **predators**. Bioluminescence is the ability of some living things to create their own light. It happens as a chemical reaction in the body. Jellyfish, some sharks, squid, and many types of fish light up in the ocean water, which can help sailors see in the dark.

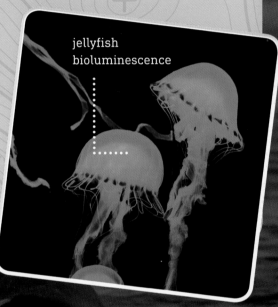

jellyfish bioluminescence

HOW TO USE A REFLECTION SIGNAL

Those stranded in the ocean can use a reflection signal to attract attention if they see a passing airplane or ship. Moving a mirror—or other shiny surface—up to eye level makes it easier to tilt it toward the Sun. This creates a small bead of light that can be seen from far away. The bead can also be used to signal a plane flying above or a ship in the distance.

A good supply of food is crucial to staying healthy at sea. Vegetables, fruit, and meat will not keep fresh for long, so canned food or preserved food is better. This includes emergency **provisions** in case the boat goes adrift. If this happens, **ration** the food and eat only if there is also drinking water. Eating makes people thirsty, and it also triggers the digestive system to use the body's water to process the food. If there is nothing to drink, sailors save water by not eating.

FOOD FROM THE SEA

Most fish in the open ocean are safe to eat. At night, plankton swims on the surface. Plankton is plentiful, **nutritious**, and easy to catch. It may be caught using a net, which can be of any fabric with very small holes. Other fish that use the lifeboat or raft for shade can also be caught. Never eat fish that smell bad or have sunken eyes and flabby skin. Puffer fish, which are found in warm, tropical seas, must be avoided because they are poisonous. Sea snakes can be eaten, but they have poisonous bites. Seaweed is full of nutrients such as vitamins and protein. It usually floats on the surface and may have small shrimp or other fish caught in it. However, it is salty and can increase thirst.

Beware of snakes such as the banded sea krait. Its poison is 10 times more powerful than that of a rattlesnake.

CATCHING BIRDS

Sea birds, such as terns, are another good source of food. Birds may fly near enough to be caught by hand or a net. Birds should always be skinned. Their feathers can be kept for **insulation**. After cutting and cleaning the bird, sailors can eat the meat immediately or preserve it. Any uneaten parts can be used as fishing **bait**.

tern ······

BE PREPARED

A knife is a very useful tool for making a fishing line and for gutting a fish. In warm places, it is best to cut the fish as soon as possible after catching it. Otherwise, it will spoil quickly. The fish can be cut into pieces and dried for eating later.

ALONE IN THE ATLANTIC:
STEVEN CALLAHAN

When Steve Callahan was 29 years old, he designed and built a boat named the *Napoleon Solo*. Steve and a friend sailed the *Solo* from Bermuda to England. Steve's plan was to take part in a race that started in England and ended in Antigua, in the Caribbean Sea. However, bad weather near Spain damaged the *Solo*. As a result, Steve had to drop out of the race.

THE JOURNEY HOME

Steve was determined to sail to the Caribbean on his boat, so he repaired the *Solo* and began his journey on his own. A few days into the trip, Steve was asleep when a violent bang shook the boat. Within seconds, the *Solo* started filling with water and began to sink.

A speargun is a useful tool for catching fish. Steve had a speargun by accident. He stored it in his raft because there was no room in the Solo's cabin.

Something had crashed into the boat, probably a whale or a shark, and made a hole in the **hull**. Steve grabbed the knife by his bunk and made it to the deck to release the inflatable lifeboat. All his supplies were in the cabin, but this was already underwater. Steve swam back and forth from the cabin to the lifeboat, gathering as many things as he could. He managed to get his sleeping bag, some water, cans of food, and an emergency kit. He had tied the raft to the *Solo*, but in a few hours, the rope became loose, and the lifeboat began drifting.

SURVIVING THE SEA

There were three **solar stills** in Steve's emergency kit. but only two worked. They produced about 20 ounces (591 ml) of water each day, so he had some fresh water to drink. For food, Steve depended on seaweed and fish. **Barnacles** collected on his raft, which attracted triggerfish and dorados, so Steve used a speargun to catch them.

One day, a dorado lashed around on his spear and tore a hole in the raft. Water started dribbling into the raft, and Steve could not make a patch stick to the wet raft. Instead, he shoved material into the hole and jammed a fork into the material to close the gap. Luckily, this sealed the hole.

LIGHTS AHEAD!

After being at sea for 76 days, Steve saw lights in the distance. He prepared to drift onto the shore, but fishermen from Marie Galante Island had seen the birds flying over Steve's raft. They knew that was a sign of many fish at that spot, so they set out. They found Steve and brought him back to shore. Steve had made his Atlantic crossing after all!

Survivors face a big problem if their boat springs a leak. Water gushes in very quickly, and there is little or no time to stop it. If there is no way to save the boat, the life raft is the only option. This, too, can leak if it is damaged by a fish or if a hook snags it. Fixing leaks of any kind is not easy to do in the middle of the ocean.

HOLE IN THE HULL

If there is water seeping into the boat, the first thing to do is to find the leak. Survivors should look for the drain plugs and make sure that they are secure. If this is not the problem, any cracks must be identified. A strip of duct tape may be able to keep most water out for long enough to go back to land. If there is a small hole in the hull, plug it as fast as possible. For an extra layer of protection, a plastic sheet can be put over the outside of the boat to help keep out water.

STAYING AFLOAT

Some sea survival equipment is similar to the adaptations that many sea animals have. For example, some bony sea fish, such as swordfish, have inflatable body parts. Like a life raft, they can be filled with air to make them bigger and then squashed flat again to make them smaller. These inflatable body parts are called swim bladders. They are little balloons that fill and deflate, or let out air, to help the fish rise or sink in the water.

LIFE RAFT REPAIR

Before setting out to sea, it is important to ensure that life rafts are undamaged. By law, life rafts must be sold with repair kits, but it is up to sailors to always make sure there is a repair kit and that it is complete. Life raft kits are supposed to work in all conditions, even when wet. Not all kits are the same. Some kits come with metal clamps that fit through a hole and seal it shut, while others have glue and patches.

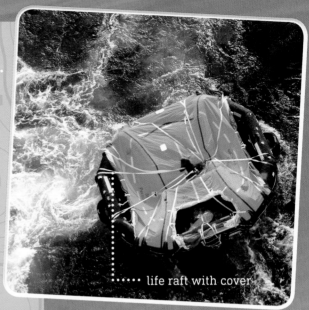

life raft with cover

The swordfish is a large predator with a long, swordlike bill. It uses it to attack prey.

BE PREPARED

Duct tape is an essential piece of equipment. Although it is useful for many jobs, fixing a leak may be the most important. Duct tape is strong and waterproof.

duct tape

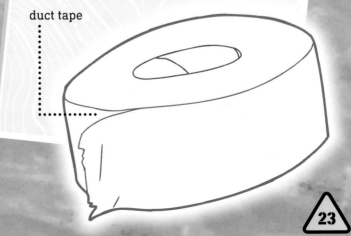

Sharks are predators, but they do not hunt humans. Even so, people on the open sea should be wary of sharks. Sharks may circle a boat in search of the fish hiding underneath. A hungry shark may also mistake a dinghy for food—and bite.

OCEAN HUNTERS

There are more than 500 different sharks in the world. The largest is the whale shark, which can grow to about 60 feet (18 m) long. This shark eats tiny sea creatures called plankton. Other sharks eat fish, squid, or seals. Sharks have good hearing, but also sense movement from far away. This helps them hunt in the dark. Sharks live in many oceans.

sharks circling beneath a boat

Great white sharks are the largest predator fish, but people are not their favorite food. They prefer other fish or sea creatures, such as seals.

HOW TO SPOT A SHARK

To figure out if it is a shark or a dolphin, look at the shape of the fin on top of the creature's body. This is the dorsal fin, and it is usually a triangle shape. In a shark, the fin might curve at the front, but it is quite straight at the back. In a dolphin, it is curved at the back. Sharks and dolphins also swim differently. A dolphin's tail makes its body move up and down. Sharks tend to move from side to side as they swim through the water.

dorsal fin

SHARK ATTACK

If a shark is nearby, always try to remain calm. Splashing around or moving suddenly will only attract the curious shark and bring it closer. If there is a spear or pole, the sailor should hold it but not move it around. If the shark does attack, the spear or pole can be used to poke at the shark's nose, eyes, and gills. This usually sends the shark swimming in the opposite direction.

NIGHTMARE AT SEA:
MAURICE AND MARALYN BAILEY

Maurice and Maralyn Bailey dreamed of sailing around the world. They sold all their belongings so they could afford to build a boat. Their plan was to sail from Southampton, England, to New Zealand. Maurice and Maralyn set sail in June 1972 on the *Auralyn*, making a few stops in Europe and then the Caribbean islands. In early 1973, the *Auralyn* passed through the Panama Canal and entered the Pacific.

HOLE IN THE HULL

What happened next changed everything. The Baileys were below deck when they felt and heard a powerful blow to the yacht. A 39-foot (12 m) sperm whale had smashed its tail into the boat's hull, causing a massive hole. Water gushed in as the Baileys frantically grabbed the rubber dinghy and a life raft. They tied the two vessels together and threw in as many supplies as they could. As their boat started to sink, they had just enough time to scramble into the raft.

STRANDED AT SEA

At first, the couple tried to row back toward land. Maurice used a sextant to figure out that they were a few hundred miles from the Galapagos Islands. They soon discovered that they were wasting their energy. Besides, the *Auralyn* was so close to the area's shipping lanes that Maurice and Maralyn were sure that they would be rescued. After eight days at sea, they saw a ship in the distance. They shot up their flares, but the ship moved on. The couple realized that they were stranded.

FINDING FOOD

The Baileys' food and water supplies were getting low. Maralyn could not find any fishing hooks among their supplies, so she attached some string to a safety pin from their first aid kit. This was good enough to catch the many triggerfish that swam by. The couple also became skilled at catching fish with their hands. Maurice and Maralyn caught sea birds, turtles, and triggerfish. Storms brought fresh water, but the violent waves were dangerous for the small raft. It was not easy to stay hopeful.

RESCUE COMES

The Baileys had been drifting for 117 days, and they were both thin and sick. On June 30, 1973, the crew of a Korean fishing boat spotted the couple and came to their rescue. Amazingly, Maurice and Maralyn did not stop sailing. Two years after their nightmare on the Pacific, they bought the *Auralyn II*. On their first trip, they set off to study whales near the coast of South America.

Many people dream of sailing the world like the Baileys. Most trips are uneventful, but it is important to always have an understanding of basic survival skills if things do go wrong.

People who have lived through sea disasters have some things in common. They used survival skills such as the ones in this book. They found fresh water and food. They kept focused by tracking the time and writing about their experiences. They dealt with the blazing Sun, terrible rains, and dangerous wildlife. Most importantly, even when everything seemed hopeless, they were determined to survive.

STAY AFLOAT

The best chances of surviving at sea include staying out of the water, if possible, then doing everything to protect the body from **exposure**. Use clothing, sails, or other coverings to protect the body from the Sun during the day and the cold at night. Over time, the saltwater spray can cause sores on skin. If possible, use a little fresh water to clean the sores to treat them and to prevent more from forming.

A coral reef is home to all kinds of fish as well as seahorses, turtles, and much more that can provide food for people.

KEEP TOGETHER

If a group is traveling on a boat, more than one life raft must be available. The rafts must be tied to the boat, if possible, or to each other. Keeping the rafts about 25 feet (7.5 m) apart will avoid damage, but they must be drawn closer together if an aircraft is nearby. It is important to look as big as possible in order to be seen. If there is no anchor to keep the raft from drifting, a roll of clothes, buoys, or other items could be attached to try and keep the raft stable. A raft can drift as much as 100 miles (160.9 km) in just one day.

BE PREPARED

If a boat is stranded north of the equator, Polaris, or the North Star, can be used to determine location. This star, above the North Pole, does not change position. To find it, look for a group of seven stars that make the shape of a ladle. This is the Big Dipper. Find the two stars that form the end of the ladle shape. Imagine a line that extends from there; this will take the eye to Polaris. Wherever sailors are in the northern hemisphere, the North Star will be at the same angle above the **horizon** as their latitude, or distance north or south from the equator.

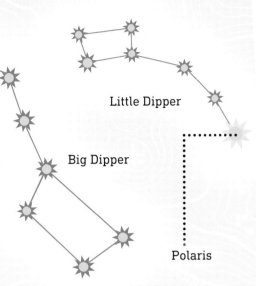

Little Dipper

Big Dipper

Polaris

Flotation devices such as life jackets must be brightly colored and the right size. If the device is too big, it will not keep the head above water.

GLOSSARY

adapted Developed skills or physical features over time to help animals live in a certain biome

bait Something used to attract and catch fish or other animals

barnacles Small sea creatures with shells that attach to hard surfaces, such as boats

biome A large area where plants and animals naturally live. A biome is also recognized by other features, such as how much water it has and what its weather is like.

buoy Floating devices that are anchored

condense When water vapor in the air cools and turns into water

currents The flow of air or water in a certain direction

dehydrates Causes excessive loss of water from a person's body

dinghy A small rubber boat

endangered Describes something that is at risk of dying out

equatorial Related to an imaginary line around the center of Earth

evaporate When liquid changes into a gas or vapor

exposure Being affected by something, such as the sun

flares Lights that shine brightly for a short time

gills A fish's breathing organ

GPS Acronym for Global Positioning System, a system that uses space satellites to help people find their way

hazards Dangerous things

horizon Where the land and sea appear to meet

hull The main part of a boat

insulation Protection against the cold

monsoons Winds in Asia that can bring heavy rain

nutritious Having substances, such as vitamins, that people or animals need to be healthy

predators Animals that hunt and eat other animals

preserve To keep something in good condition

prey Animals that are hunted and killed by other animals for food

provisions Supplies of food and other things that will be needed

pyrotechnic Fireworks, such as flares

ration To allow only so much per person at one time

sextant An instrument that measures the positions of the stars and Sun. Used for navigation at sea.

solar stills Devices for purifying water. They use sunlight to make water evaporate and then condense.

SOS A universal rescue signal that stands for Save Our Souls

typhoon A tropical storm that develops in the northwest Pacific Ocean

LEARNING MORE

Find out more about oceans and how to survive them.

Bell, Samantha. *How to Survive Being Lost at Sea* (Survival Guides). Child's World, 2015.

Ishak, Lauren. *Map and Track Oceans* (Map and Track Biomes and Animals). Crabtree Publishing, 2019.

Martin, Claudia. *Make It Out Alive in the Ocean* (Makerspace Survival). PowerKids Press, 2017.

Wilsdon, Christina. *Ultimate Oceanpedia*. National Geographic Kids, 2016.

WEBSITES

Learn more about the ocean biome at:
https://kids.nationalgeographic.com/explore/nature/habitats/ocean

Find out all about ocean wildlife at:
https://ocean.si.edu/ocean-life

Discover more about survivor stories at:
www.bbc.com/news/world-39783347

Read more about boat safety at:
www.discoverboating.com/resources/boat-safety-checklist-safety-equipment

INDEX

ABOUT THE AUTHOR

Cynthia O'Brien has written many books about nature. She has traveled to different parts of the world but has never been on the open ocean. Writing this book, she learned a lot more about the ocean biome. If she goes on an ocean trip, she now knows a lot more about how to prepare and some lifesaving tips.